Copyright Reserved

Contents

BUSINESS PLANNING AND PROPOSALS BOOK FOR BEGINNER 2024

Unleashing the Power of Strategic Business Planning and Irresistible Proposals for Unprecedented Growth

BY

EDEN WALKER

2024
BUSINESS PLANNING
&
PROPOSAL
BOOK
EDWEN WALKER

Chapter 1: Introduction to Business Planning

1.0 Introduction

Embarking on the entrepreneurial journey is akin to setting sail on an uncharted sea, where the destination is clear, but the path is fraught with challenges and opportunities. As you stand on the precipice of possibility, envisioning the growth of your business, the importance of a well-crafted business plan becomes your guiding star. This chapter is the threshold to a comprehensive exploration of business planning—an essential compass for every aspiring entrepreneur.

1.1 Setting Sail: A Captivating Prelude

Picture this: A visionary entrepreneur, Sarah, found herself at the helm of a revolutionary idea that could reshape the landscape of her industry. The yearning to turn her vision into reality ignited a spark within her, prompting her to navigate uncharted waters. Yet, as the winds of uncertainty whispered doubts, Sarah realized the need for a roadmap—a business plan that would not only guide her but also attract potential investors and collaborators.

Sarah's journey mirrors the quintessential entrepreneurial spirit, where dreams collide with the practicalities of execution. In the bustling cityscape, she sought out mentors who shared tales of triumphs and pitfalls. One name echoed in every conversation—George Teller, a seasoned entrepreneur whose success was rooted in meticulous business planning.

1.2 The Lure of Business Planning

Business planning is more than a mere roadmap; it is a compass that aligns your aspirations with strategic precision. In this chapter, we delve into the fundamental purpose and importance of business planning. It's not just about numbers and projections; it's about sculpting a vision into a tangible, viable entity.

1.3 Unveiling the Business Plan Components

A business plan is a mosaic of interconnected elements. Each piece plays a crucial role in painting a vivid picture of your venture. We unravel these components, from the executive summary to the financial forecast, unveiling their significance in transforming a mere concept into a compelling business narrative.

As we embark on this exploration, remember: Your business plan is not just a document; it's a narrative that captivates stakeholders, instills confidence, and sets the stage for success. The chapters that follow will be your guide through the intricate art of business planning, equipping you with the knowledge to navigate the unpredictable currents of entrepreneurship. Welcome to the world where ideas take flight, guided by the wings of a well-crafted business plan.

As you embark on crafting your business plan, it's crucial to understand the distinct components that form the foundation of this comprehensive document. Each element serves a unique purpose, contributing to the overall narrative of your venture.

1.3.1 Executive Summary: The Beacon of Conciseness

At the helm of your business plan stands the executive summary, a concise yet powerful overview of your entire business. Think of it as the beacon that draws in potential investors and partners. In this section, distill the essence of your venture, outlining its mission, unique value proposition, and the market opportunity it addresses. Despite its brevity, the executive summary sets the tone for the entire document.

1.3.2 Company Overview: Crafting Your Identity

Your company overview is the canvas on which you paint the identity of your business. Dive into the history, mission, vision, and values that define your enterprise. Share the story behind its inception, instilling a sense of purpose that resonates with stakeholders. This section is where your business takes shape, transitioning from a concept to a distinct entity.

1.3.3 Market Analysis: Navigating the Business Landscape

The market analysis is your compass in the sea of competition. Dive deep into market research, identifying trends, opportunities, and potential challenges. Understand your target customers—their needs, preferences, and behaviors. Analyze the competitive landscape, mapping out your position in the market ecosystem. This section equips you with the knowledge needed to make informed strategic decisions.

1.3.4 Business Structure and Organization: Building the Foundation

Just as a ship needs a sturdy hull, your business requires a solid structure. Outline your organizational setup, detailing the hierarchy, roles, and responsibilities. Define the legal structure of your business, whether it's a sole proprietorship, partnership, LLC, or corporation. This section provides clarity on the internal workings of your venture, fostering efficiency and accountability.

1.3.5 Products or Services: The Heart of Your Offering

Your products or services are the beating heart of your business. Unveil the details of what you offer, emphasizing the unique features and benefits that set you apart. Clearly articulate your value proposition, demonstrating how your offerings meet the needs of your target market. This section is your opportunity to showcase the excellence that defines your brand.

1.3.6 Marketing and Sales Strategy: Charting the Course to Success

In this section, chart a course for how you plan to market and sell your products or services. Define your target audience, outline your promotional strategies, and elucidate your sales approach. A well-crafted marketing and sales strategy not only attracts customers but also showcases your understanding of the market dynamics.

1.3.7 Financial Plan: Navigating the Fiscal Waters

The financial plan is the compass that steers your business toward financial success. Dive into budgeting, revenue projections, and expense forecasts. Explore funding options, detailing how you plan to secure the necessary capital. Whether you're seeking investors or opting for self-funding, this section provides a clear financial roadmap for your venture.

1.3.8 Risk Analysis and Mitigation: Safeguarding Your Voyage

Every journey involves risks, and the business landscape is no exception. Identify potential risks and uncertainties that could impact your venture. Develop strategies for risk mitigation, showcasing your proactive approach to challenges. This section instills confidence in stakeholders, demonstrating your ability to navigate turbulent waters with resilience.

As you embark on the exploration of these business plan components, remember that each piece contributes to the holistic narrative of your venture. Together, they create a compelling story that captivates stakeholders and charts a course for the success of your entrepreneurial journey.

CHAPTER 2   Market Analysis

In the vast sea of business, understanding the currents of the market is paramount. Market analysis serves as the navigational chart, guiding entrepreneurs through the intricacies of consumer behavior, industry trends, and competitive landscapes. In this chapter, we embark on a journey to dissect market analysis, illuminating its significance and providing practical insights to equip you for the dynamic waters of business.

2.1 Conducting Market Research: The Foundation of Informed Decision-Making

Market research is the bedrock of any successful business venture. It involves gathering, analyzing, and interpreting information about the market, consumers, and competitors. Imagine a scenario where you're launching a new line of organic skincare products. Before diving into production, thorough market research would involve understanding the demand for organic products, consumer preferences, and competitor offerings.

Practical Example:

Let's say your market research reveals a rising trend in eco-conscious consumers seeking chemical-free skincare. This insight not only validates your product idea but also allows you to tailor your offerings to meet the specific demands of your target audience.

2.2 Identifying Target Customers: Crafting Personas for Precision

Knowing your target customers is like setting your sails in the right direction. Create detailed customer personas that go beyond demographics to capture behaviors, motivations, and pain points. Returning to the skincare example, your target customers might include environmentally conscious millennials who prioritize cruelty-free and sustainable products.

millennials who prioritize cruelty-free and sustainable products.

Practical Example:

By identifying your target customers, you can tailor your marketing messages and product features to resonate with their values. This might involve using recyclable packaging, emphasizing cruelty-free testing, and highlighting the natural ingredients in your skincare line.

2.3 Analyzing Competitor Landscape: Understanding the Chessboard of Business

Business is often a strategic game, and understanding your competitors is akin to studying your opponents on a chessboard. Analyze not only direct competitors but also indirect players who might impact your market share. In the skincare realm, your competitors extend beyond other organic brands to include mainstream products that might pivot towards eco-friendly alternatives.

Practical Example:

If a major competitor announces plans to launch a similar line of organic skincare, your analysis should include predicting potential shifts in market dynamics. This foresight allows you to adapt your marketing strategy, perhaps emphasizing unique selling points or adjusting pricing to maintain a competitive edge.

Market analysis is not a one-time endeavor but an ongoing process that adapts to the dynamic nature of business. Regularly revisit your research to stay attuned to evolving consumer preferences, emerging trends, and shifts in the competitive landscape. This adaptive approach positions your business to ride the waves of change rather than being swept away by them.

As you navigate the waters of market analysis, remember that knowledge is your compass. The insights gained through thorough research empower you to make informed decisions, mitigating risks and steering your business towards sustainable growth. In the next chapters, we delve into strategic planning, financial considerations, and operational intricacies, building upon the foundation laid by a robust market analysis.

Chapter 3: Strategic Planning

Strategic planning is the helm that guides a business toward its envisioned destination. It involves setting goals, crafting a roadmap, and making decisions that align with a long-term vision. In this chapter, we delve into the art and science of strategic planning, exploring its core components and offering practical examples to illuminate its application in the dynamic world of business.

3.1 Developing a Business Strategy: The Blueprint for Success

At the core of strategic planning is the development of a robust business strategy. This blueprint outlines how an organization will achieve its goals and gain a competitive advantage. Imagine you are the founder of a tech startup aiming to disrupt the e-learning industry. Your strategy might involve leveraging cutting-edge technology to provide personalized learning experiences.

Practical Example:

By developing a strategy that integrates artificial intelligence for adaptive learning modules, you not only differentiate your platform but also address the evolving needs of students. This approach positions your startup as an innovative player in the competitive e-learning landscape.

3.2 SWOT Analysis: Navigating Strengths, Weaknesses, Opportunities, and Threats

A SWOT analysis is a strategic tool that assesses a company's internal strengths and weaknesses, along with external opportunities and threats. This introspective process provides a holistic view of the business environment. Consider a scenario where you run a small bakery. Identifying strengths like unique recipes and a loyal customer base is crucial, but so is acknowledging weaknesses such as limited marketing resources.

Practical Example:

Conducting a SWOT analysis might reveal an opportunity to collaborate with a local coffee shop to expand your customer reach. Simultaneously, recognizing the threat of increasing competition in your neighborhood prompts strategic measures, like introducing new product lines or enhancing customer experience, to maintain your market position.

3.3 Creating Competitive Advantage: Unleashing the Unique Proposition

In the vast sea of business, a competitive advantage is the wind in your sails—a unique proposition that distinguishes your offerings from competitors. Consider a scenario where you're managing a boutique graphic design agency. Your competitive advantage might stem from a combination of highly skilled designers, a rapid turnaround time, and personalized client relationships.

Practical Example:

Emphasizing your agency's ability to deliver high-quality designs within tight deadlines positions you as a reliable choice for clients with time-sensitive projects. This competitive advantage becomes a key element of your marketing strategy, setting you apart in a crowded market.

Strategic planning is not a static process but an iterative one that adapts to the evolving business landscape. Regularly reassess your strategy in light of market changes, technological advancements, and shifts in consumer behavior. The ability to pivot strategically ensures your business remains agile and responsive.

As you navigate the waters of strategic planning, remember that it's a dynamic dance between vision and execution. The strategic choices you make today shape the course of your business tomorrow. In the subsequent chapters, we delve into the financial intricacies of your plan, operational considerations, and the art of effective marketing. Together, these elements harmonize to orchestrate the success of your strategic endeavors.

Chapter 4: Financial Planning

Financial planning is the compass that directs the course of your business voyage. It involves forecasting, budgeting, and allocating resources to achieve your strategic objectives. In this chapter, we delve into the intricacies of financial planning, exploring key components and providing practical examples to illuminate its critical role in steering your business toward sustainable success.

4.1 Budgeting and Forecasting: Navigating the Fiscal Waters

Budgeting and forecasting are the anchors of financial planning, providing a structured framework to allocate resources and anticipate future financial outcomes. Imagine you're the owner of a small retail business. Effective budgeting involves meticulously planning expenses, such as rent, utilities, and inventory costs, while forecasting anticipates potential sales based on historical data and market trends.

Practical Example:

By creating a detailed budget, you gain visibility into your financial health, enabling proactive management of cash flow. Additionally, accurate forecasting allows you to adjust inventory levels in response to seasonal demand fluctuations, preventing overstock or shortages.

4.2 Financial Statements: The Ledger of Business Health

Financial statements are the heartbeat of your business, conveying its fiscal health to stakeholders. The three main statements—income statement, balance sheet, and cash flow statement—provide a comprehensive overview. Picture yourself as the founder of a software development startup. Your income statement details revenue and expenses, illustrating the profitability of your services.

Practical Example:

Analyzing the income statement might reveal that software development projects generate substantial revenue, but marketing expenses are high. Armed with this insight, you can make informed decisions, such as optimizing marketing strategies to improve cost-effectiveness without compromising client acquisition.

4.3 Funding Options and Capital Structure: Sourcing the Financial Wind

Understanding funding options and capital structure is akin to choosing the sails that propel your business forward. Different stages of your business may require diverse funding sources, from personal savings and loans to angel investors or venture capital. Consider a scenario where you're expanding a tech startup. Initially, bootstrapping or seeking seed funding may be viable. As your venture grows, you might explore additional funding through venture capital to fuel expansion.

Practical Example:

Optimizing your capital structure involves balancing equity and debt. If your startup secures a significant venture capital investment, you may choose to use debt strategically for specific growth initiatives, maintaining a balanced and sustainable capital structure that aligns with your long-term goals.

Financial planning is not a one-size-fits-all process but a tailored strategy that evolves with the dynamics of your business. Regularly review and adjust your financial plan in response to market changes, business growth, or unforeseen challenges. This adaptive approach ensures your financial compass remains true even in turbulent fiscal waters.

As you navigate the financial intricacies of your business, remember that sound financial planning is a strategic advantage. It not only safeguards your business against uncertainties but also positions it for growth and resilience. In the upcoming chapters, we explore the operational aspects of your plan, delve into marketing strategies, and guide you through the implementation and monitoring phases of your entrepreneurial journey. Together, these elements harmonize to orchestrate the success of your business vision.

Chapter 5: Operational Planning

Operational planning is the engine that propels your business forward, converting strategic objectives into tangible actions. It involves designing efficient processes, managing resources, and mitigating risks. In this chapter, we navigate through the intricacies of operational planning, exploring its key components and providing practical examples to illuminate its pivotal role in the seamless functioning of your business.

5.1 Designing Efficient Business Processes: The Blueprint for Productivity

Efficient business processes are the foundation of operational excellence. Imagine you run a small e-commerce business. Designing an efficient order fulfillment process involves streamlining steps from receiving an order to shipping the product. This might include automated inventory management, a user-friendly online ordering system, and strategic partnerships with reliable shipping providers.

Practical Example:

By optimizing the order fulfillment process, you reduce errors, enhance customer satisfaction, and increase overall productivity. Efficiency in business processes not only saves time and resources but also positions your business for scalability.

5.2 Supply Chain Management: Navigating the Flow of Goods and Services

Supply chain management is the intricate dance of sourcing, producing, and delivering products or services. Picture yourself as the owner of a food distribution company. Effective supply chain management involves sourcing quality ingredients, optimizing production schedules, and ensuring timely delivery to clients.

Practical Example:

Implementing just-in-time inventory practices can minimize storage costs and reduce the risk of product spoilage. This approach ensures that products are ordered and delivered precisely when needed, optimizing the supply chain for both efficiency and cost-effectiveness.

5.3 Risk Assessment and Mitigation: Safeguarding Your Business Voyage

Every business voyage encounters storms, and risk assessment and mitigation are the lifebuoys that keep your ship afloat. Consider a scenario where you manage a software development company. Identifying potential risks, such as cybersecurity threats or project delays, allows you to implement proactive measures. This might include regular security audits, contingency plans, and diversifying project timelines.

Practical Example:

By conducting a thorough risk assessment, you anticipate challenges and prepare mitigation strategies. This proactive approach minimizes the impact of unforeseen events, ensuring that your business sails through uncertainties with resilience.

Operational planning is not a static blueprint but a dynamic process that evolves with the changing tides of your business environment. Regularly reassess and refine your operational plan to accommodate growth, technological advancements, and shifts in consumer expectations. This adaptive approach ensures your operations remain agile and responsive.

As you navigate the operational intricacies of your business, remember that operational efficiency is not merely a cost-cutting measure but a strategic advantage. It enhances customer satisfaction, improves employee morale, and positions your business for sustained success. In the upcoming chapters, we explore marketing and sales strategies, guide you through the art of proposal writing, and unveil the implementation and monitoring phases of your entrepreneurial journey. Together, these elements harmonize to orchestrate the success of your business vision.

Chapter 6: Marketing and Sales Strategies

In the bustling marketplace, where every business competes for attention, effective marketing and sales strategies are the wind that fills your entrepreneurial sails. This chapter delves into the art and science of marketing and sales, exploring key strategies and providing practical examples to illuminate their transformative impact on your business.

6.1 Crafting Effective Marketing Plans: The Art of Visibility

Your marketing plan is the compass that guides customers to your doorstep. Picture yourself as the owner of a local coffee shop. Crafting an effective marketing plan involves understanding your target audience, utilizing various channels such as social media, local events, and partnerships to create visibility, and defining key messages that resonate with your audience.

Practical Example:

If your target audience includes young professionals, you might leverage Instagram and Facebook to showcase your coffee shop's ambiance, specialty drinks, and promotions. Engaging content, coupled with strategic advertising, can increase brand awareness and draw in your desired customer demographic.

6.2 Sales Tactics and Customer Acquisition: The Art of Persuasion

Sales tactics are the sails that propel your business forward, turning potential leads into loyal customers. Imagine you run a software company specializing in project management tools. Your sales tactics might involve personalized demonstrations, free trial offers, and a tiered pricing structure that caters to businesses of different sizes.

Practical Example:

Offering a free trial allows potential customers to experience the value of your software firsthand. During personalized demonstrations, emphasize how your product addresses their specific pain points. A tiered pricing structure accommodates diverse customer needs, ensuring that businesses of varying scales can benefit from your software.

6.3 Building a Brand Identity: The Lighthouse in a Sea of Choices

In the vast sea of consumer choices, a strong brand identity serves as a lighthouse, guiding customers to your business amidst the waves of competition. Consider yourself as the founder of a sustainable clothing brand. Building a brand identity involves defining your brand values, creating a distinctive visual identity, and consistently communicating your brand story.

Practical Example:

If sustainability is a core value, your brand identity might emphasize eco-friendly practices, ethical sourcing, and transparent manufacturing processes. This resonates with environmentally conscious consumers, creating a unique brand positioning in the market.

Marketing and sales strategies are not isolated endeavors but interconnected elements of a holistic approach to customer engagement. Integrating these strategies ensures a seamless and impactful customer journey, from initial awareness to conversion and long-term loyalty.

As you navigate the marketing and sales waters of your business, remember that authenticity and consistency are the North Star. Build genuine connections with your audience, stay true to your brand values, and adapt your strategies based on customer feedback and market trends. In the upcoming chapters, we explore the art of proposal writing, the nuances of implementation and monitoring, and the critical aspects of continuous improvement. Together, these elements harmonize to orchestrate the success of your business vision.

Chapter 7: Proposal Writing

In the realm of business, the ability to articulate your ideas persuasively is as crucial as the quality of those ideas. Proposal writing is the craft of transforming concepts into compelling narratives that resonate with potential stakeholders. This chapter delves into the intricacies of proposal writing, exploring its significance and providing a detailed guide to creating winning proposals.

7.1 Understanding Proposal Requirements: The Foundation of Success

Before the ink touches the paper or the digital document takes form, understanding the intricacies of proposal requirements is paramount. Whether responding to a request for proposal (RFP) or initiating a proposal independently, clarity on expectations is the foundation of success. Consider a scenario where you're a graphic design agency bidding for a contract. Understanding the client's aesthetic preferences, project scope, and specific deliverables is crucial in crafting a proposal that aligns seamlessly with their vision.

Practical Example:

If the client emphasizes a preference for minimalist designs and quick turnaround times, incorporating these specifics into your proposal demonstrates attentiveness to their needs, setting the stage for a mutually beneficial partnership.

7.2 Structuring a Winning Proposal: The Architecture of Persuasion

A winning proposal is more than a compilation of ideas; it is a structured narrative that captures attention and convinces stakeholders of the value you bring. Crafting a compelling structure involves several key components:

Executive Summary: A concise overview of the proposal, highlighting key points and enticing the reader to delve deeper.

Introduction: Setting the stage by providing context, addressing the client's pain points, and establishing your understanding of their needs.

Objectives and Goals: Clearly articulating the objectives of the proposal and outlining the goals you aim to achieve.

Methodology or Approach: Detailing the step-by-step plan or methodology you propose to achieve the objectives.

Timeline: Providing a realistic timeline for project milestones, demonstrating your commitment to timely delivery.

Budget: Transparently presenting the financial aspects, including a breakdown of costs, ensuring alignment with the client's expectations.

Credentials and Experience: Showcasing your team's expertise, relevant experience, and successful projects to instill confidence in your capabilities.

Conclusion: Reinforcing key points, expressing enthusiasm for the collaboration, and encouraging further discussion

Practical Example:

For a marketing agency responding to an RFP, structuring the proposal involves not only presenting creative campaign ideas but also substantiating them with market research, showcasing past successful campaigns, and detailing a realistic timeline and budget.

7.3 Incorporating Persuasive Writing Techniques: The Art of Influence

Beyond the structure lies the art of persuasive writing—capturing the hearts and minds of your audience. Here are some techniques to infuse persuasion into your proposal:

Clear and Concise Language: Communicate ideas with clarity and brevity, avoiding unnecessary jargon or complexity.

Storytelling: Weave a narrative that resonates emotionally, emphasizing the human side of your proposal.

Addressing Pain Points: Demonstrate a deep understanding of the client's challenges and position your proposal as the solution.

Benefits-Oriented Language: Focus on the benefits and outcomes rather than just features, showing how your proposal adds value.

Evidence and Testimonials: Incorporate case studies, testimonials, or data to substantiate your claims and build credibility.

Call-to-Action: Clearly outline the next steps and encourage the client to take action, fostering a proactive response.

Practical Example:

In a proposal for a technology upgrade project, persuasive writing might involve emphasizing not just the technical specifications of the new system but also the positive impact on efficiency, cost savings, and user experience, supported by testimonials from previous clients who benefited from similar upgrades.

Proposal writing is an art that requires a delicate blend of strategic thinking, effective communication, and a keen understanding of the audience. As you embark on crafting proposals for your business endeavors, remember that each proposal is a unique opportunity to showcase your capabilities and forge meaningful partnerships.

In the subsequent chapters, we navigate through the implementation and monitoring phases of your business plan, exploring the practicalities of turning proposals into tangible actions. Together, these elements harmonize to orchestrate the success of your business vision.

Chapter 8: Implementation and Monitoring

With a well-crafted business plan, strategic insights, and compelling proposals, you've set the stage for success. However, the true measure of your entrepreneurial journey lies in the implementation of your plans and the vigilant monitoring of your progress. This chapter delves into the critical phases of implementation and monitoring, exploring the practicalities and providing comprehensive guidance for turning your business vision into reality.

8.1 Executing the Business Plan: Turning Vision into Action

The execution phase is the heartbeat of your business plan. It involves translating strategic intentions into tangible actions, aligning teams, and navigating the intricacies of day-to-day operations. Consider a scenario where you are the founder of a software development company aiming to launch a groundbreaking product. Executing the business plan involves:

Team Alignment: Ensure that your team understands the strategic goals, has clarity on individual roles, and is committed to the overarching vision.

Operationalization: Put your business processes into action, from production and service delivery to customer support and administrative functions.

Technology Integration: Implement the necessary technologies to support your operations, whether it's project management tools, customer relationship management (CRM) systems, or communication platforms.

Marketing and Sales Activation: Launch your marketing campaigns, activate your sales strategies, and engage with your target audience.

Practical Example:

In the case of the software development company, executing the business plan involves the collaborative effort of developers, marketers, and sales teams. The launch includes deploying the product, initiating marketing campaigns across digital platforms, and activating sales channels to reach potential clients.

8.2 Key Performance Indicators (KPIs): Quantifying Success Metrics

As you set sail in the sea of implementation, navigating without instruments can lead to uncertainty. Key Performance Indicators (KPIs) act as your navigational tools, quantifying success metrics and providing insights into the effectiveness of your strategies. These could include:

Financial KPIs: Revenue growth, profit margins, and return on investment (ROI).

Operational KPIs: Efficiency ratios, production output, and resource utilization.

Marketing KPIs: Conversion rates, customer acquisition costs, and brand engagement.

Customer Success KPIs: Retention rates, customer satisfaction scores, and net promoter scores (NPS).

Practical Example:

For an e-commerce business, financial KPIs might involve tracking monthly revenue, operational KPIs could include order fulfillment times, marketing KPIs might focus on customer acquisition costs, and customer success KPIs may include measuring customer satisfaction through surveys.

3 Continuous Improvement Strategies: Navigating the Winds of Change

In the dynamic business environment, adaptation is the key to sustained success. Continuous improvement involves an iterative process of refinement based on insights gathered during implementation and monitoring. Strategies for continuous improvement include:

Feedback Loops: Establish mechanisms for collecting feedback from customers, employees, and stakeholders, and use this information to make informed adjustments.

Performance Reviews: Regularly assess the performance of your strategies against KPIs, identifying areas of improvement and opportunities for optimization.

Market Research: Stay attuned to shifts in the market, emerging trends, and changing consumer behaviors, adapting your strategies to align with evolving dynamics.

Employee Development: Invest in the growth and development of your team, ensuring that they stay equipped with the skills and knowledge needed for optimal performance.

Practical Example:

For a restaurant business, continuous improvement might involve analyzing customer feedback to refine the menu, conducting performance reviews to optimize kitchen efficiency, staying updated on culinary trends through market research, and providing ongoing training for staff to enhance service quality.

8.4 Case Study: The Implementation and Monitoring Journey of XYZ Tech Solutions

Let's delve into a case study to bring the concepts of implementation and monitoring to life. XYZ Tech Solutions, a software development company, aimed to launch a cutting-edge project management tool. Their journey unfolded in the following stages:

Strategic Planning: XYZ Tech Solutions conducted extensive market research to identify the need for a user-friendly project management tool with advanced collaboration features.

Proposal Writing: They crafted a compelling proposal for potential clients, highlighting the unique features of their tool, showcasing testimonials from beta testing, and detailing a phased implementation plan.

Implementation: The team at XYZ Tech Solutions initiated a phased launch of their project management tool, starting with a beta version to gather user feedback before the full-scale release. They aligned their development, marketing, and sales teams to ensure a cohesive and synchronized launch.

Monitoring: Utilizing KPIs such as user engagement, conversion rates, and customer satisfaction scores, XYZ Tech Solutions continuously monitored the performance of their tool. They actively sought feedback through user surveys and conducted regular team meetings to assess progress.

Continuous Improvement: Based on feedback and performance reviews, XYZ Tech Solutions implemented updates to enhance user experience, introduced new features in response to market trends, and invested in ongoing employee training to maintain a high level of customer support.

This case study illustrates how a business navigated through the phases of implementation and monitoring, utilizing strategic planning, effective proposal writing, and a commitment to continuous improvement.

As you embark on the implementation and monitoring phases of your business plan, remember that flexibility, resilience, and a commitment to continuous improvement are your compass and sails. The ability to adapt to changing winds, steer through uncertainties, and optimize your course based on real-time insights will determine the success of your entrepreneurial voyage.

In the upcoming chapters, we explore the nuances of marketing and sales strategies, guide you through the art of proposal writing, and unveil the critical aspects of implementation and monitoring. Together, these elements harmonize to orchestrate the success of your business vision.

Chapter 9: Scaling Heights - The Art of Business Expansion

As your entrepreneurial voyage gains momentum, the horizon expands, beckoning you to scale new heights. Chapter 9 is a pivotal chapter that delves into the art of business expansion. Discover the strategies, challenges, and triumphs associated with taking your enterprise to the next level.

9.1 Strategic Growth Initiatives: Charting the Course for Expansion

Strategic growth is the compass that guides your business into unexplored territories. Consider a scenario where you manage a successful e-commerce platform specializing in handmade crafts. Strategic growth initiatives might involve expanding your product line, entering new markets, or forming partnerships with artisans to enhance your offerings.

Practical Example:

By introducing a line of eco-friendly crafts sourced from artisans in different regions, you not only diversify your product range but also tap into a broader market of environmentally conscious consumers.

9.2 International Expansion: Navigating Global Waters

International expansion is a thrilling chapter that invites you to navigate the global business landscape. Imagine you own a tech startup with innovative software solutions. International expansion might involve establishing partnerships with overseas distributors, customizing your software to cater to specific global markets, and navigating regulatory frameworks in different countries.

Practical Example:

Expanding into the European market could involve adapting your software to comply with GDPR regulations, partnering with local tech distributors, and tailoring your marketing strategy to resonate with the diverse cultural preferences of European consumers.

9.3 Franchise Models: Replicating Success

The franchise model is a proven script for scaling success. If you've developed a successful business with a unique and replicable concept, franchising can be the key to widespread expansion. Consider a thriving fast-food restaurant. Implementing a franchise model allows entrepreneurs in different locations to replicate your successful business model, fostering brand consistency while tapping into local markets.

Practical Example:

A fast-food franchise might attract aspiring entrepreneurs who are passionate about the brand's offerings. Through a franchise agreement, they receive support, branding, and operational guidelines to ensure uniformity across various locations.

9.4 Case Study: XYZ Apparel's Global Triumph

Let's delve into a case study to bring the concept of business expansion to life. XYZ Apparel, a successful fashion brand, aimed to expand its reach globally:

Strategic Growth: XYZ Apparel identified a growing demand for sustainable fashion and decided to expand its product line to include a sustainable collection, aligning with emerging market trends.

International Expansion: Recognizing the potential in the Asian market, XYZ Apparel strategically entered partnerships with local distributors, adapted its sizing and styles to suit cultural preferences, and launched targeted marketing campaigns to establish a strong presence in Asia.

Franchise Models: Capitalizing on its brand recognition, XYZ Apparel introduced a franchise model, allowing entrepreneurs in different countries to open XYZ Apparel stores. Franchisees received comprehensive support, including marketing materials, product guidelines, and training, ensuring a consistent brand experience across the globe.

This Chapter propels your entrepreneurial narrative into a thrilling sequel, where growth knows no bounds. Whether through strategic initiatives, international endeavors, or franchising, the art of business expansion is about conquering new horizons while maintaining the essence of what made your business a success.

As you turn the pages of Chapter 9, envision the possibilities that await your business on the global stage. Embrace the challenges, learn from practical examples, and let the art of expansion be the crescendo in your entrepreneurial symphony.

In the upcoming chapters, we explore the intricacies of leadership, delve into the transformative power of innovation, and guide you through the nuances of sustainability in business. Together, these elements harmonize to orchestrate the continued success of your entrepreneurial vision.

Chapter 10: Leadership Excellence - Navigating the Entrepreneurial Ship

In the vast expanse of entrepreneurial waters, effective leadership stands as the guiding force that steers the ship through both calm seas and turbulent storms. Chapter 10 is a compass that directs your attention to the intricacies of leadership excellence, exploring the qualities, challenges, and strategies essential for captaining your entrepreneurial vessel.

10.1 The Essence of Leadership: Charting the Course

Leadership is not merely a title; it's a commitment to inspiring, guiding, and empowering your team. Imagine yourself as the captain of a ship. Effective leadership involves setting a clear course, communicating the vision, and instilling a sense of purpose among your crew. Consider a scenario where you lead a tech startup. Your role as a leader might involve fostering a culture of innovation, encouraging open communication, and aligning your team with the company's mission.

Practical Example:

By regularly communicating the company's vision for creating cutting-edge solutions, fostering an environment where ideas are valued, and leading by example in embracing innovation, you inspire your team to work towards shared goals.

10.2 Adaptive Leadership: Navigating Change

In the dynamic seas of entrepreneurship, change is the only constant. Adaptive leadership is the rudder that allows your ship to navigate through evolving tides. As the leader, you must be agile, responsive, and capable of steering your team through uncertainties. Picture yourself at the helm of a retail business facing shifts in consumer preferences. Adaptive leadership involves staying attuned to market trends, adjusting product offerings, and ensuring your team is equipped to embrace change.

Practical Example:

If your retail business traditionally focused on in-store sales, adaptive leadership might involve swiftly transitioning to e-commerce platforms in response to changing consumer behavior. This adaptability ensures your business remains relevant and resilient in the face of market shifts.

10.3 Servant Leadership: Empowering the Crew

Servant leadership is the wind in your sails, emphasizing a leader's role in serving and empowering their team. In this leadership model, the captain is not just a commander but a servant to the crew, fostering a collaborative and supportive environment. Consider leading a team of professionals in a consulting firm. Servant leadership involves providing the resources and support needed for your team to excel, removing obstacles in their path, and fostering a culture of mutual respect and cooperation.

Practical Example:

As a servant leader, you might invest in professional development opportunities for your team, ensure they have the necessary tools and resources to excel, and actively listen to their concerns and suggestions. This approach creates a positive and empowered team dynamic.

10.4 Case Study: Leadership Odyssey of XYZ Tech Solutions

Let's delve into the story of XYZ Tech Solutions, a software development company, to illuminate the principles of leadership excellence:

The Essence of Leadership: The founder of XYZ Tech Solutions, as a visionary leader, instilled a culture of innovation and collaboration. Regular team meetings, where the company's mission and goals were communicated, created a shared sense of purpose among the team.

Adaptive Leadership: When faced with a rapidly changing tech landscape, XYZ Tech Solutions' leadership swiftly adapted by investing in ongoing training for its developers, ensuring they stayed abreast of emerging technologies. This proactive approach positioned the company as a leader in cutting-edge solutions.

Servant Leadership: The CEO of XYZ Tech Solutions embraced servant leadership by actively engaging with the development team, understanding their challenges, and providing the necessary resources for their success. This approach cultivated a culture of trust and collaboration, where team members felt empowered to contribute their best.

10.5 Transformational Leadership: Inspiring Greatness

Transformational leadership is the beacon that inspires greatness among your team. It goes beyond managing day-to-day tasks; it involves igniting a passion for excellence and fostering an environment where individuals can reach their full potential. Picture leading a creative agency. Transformational leadership involves encouraging bold ideas, recognizing and celebrating achievements, and creating a workplace culture where innovation flourishes.

Practical Example:

By acknowledging and rewarding creative achievements, providing opportunities for skill development, and consistently communicating a vision of groundbreaking projects, a transformational leader in a creative agency motivates the team to surpass their own expectations and create exceptional work.

10.6 Authentic Leadership: Guided by Integrity

Authentic leadership is the North Star that guides your entrepreneurial ship with integrity and transparency. As a leader, being authentic involves aligning your actions with your values, fostering trust, and establishing genuine connections with your team. Imagine leading a socially responsible business. Authentic leadership requires not just promoting sustainability in products but ensuring the entire business operates ethically and transparently.

Practical Example:

An authentic leader in a socially responsible business would not only champion eco-friendly products but also ensure ethical sourcing, fair labor practices, and transparent communication with customers. This authenticity builds a strong foundation of trust and loyalty.

10.7 Emotional Intelligence: Navigating the Human Element

In the intricate dance of leadership, emotional intelligence is the skill that allows you to navigate the complexities of human interactions. It involves understanding and managing your own emotions, as well as empathizing with and influencing the emotions of others. Consider leading a customer service team. Emotional intelligence involves recognizing the stressors of frontline employees, providing emotional support, and fostering a positive and empathetic customer service environment.

Practical Example:

An emotionally intelligent leader might implement regular check-ins to gauge the emotional well-being of the team, offer resources for stress management, and actively listen to customer service representatives' feedback to address concerns and improve their work environment.

CONCLUSION

In conclusion, the process of business planning and proposal development is a multifaceted and crucial aspect of any successful enterprise. This book has aimed to provide a comprehensive guide, offering insights and methodologies that businesses can leverage to enhance their strategic planning and proposal creation.

First and foremost, the importance of a well-crafted business plan cannot be overstated. It serves as the roadmap for the organization, providing a clear direction, purpose, and set of goals. Through the various steps outlined in this book, from conducting market research to defining business objectives, businesses can establish a solid foundation for sustainable growth and success.

The proposal development section of this book delves into the intricacies of presenting a compelling case for a business idea, project, or partnership. A meticulously crafted proposal not only communicates the value proposition effectively but also instills confidence in potential stakeholders, investors, and collaborators. The insights shared in this book, ranging from structuring proposals to incorporating persuasive language, are designed to empower businesses in making impactful presentations.

Furthermore, the emphasis on adaptability and flexibility throughout the planning and proposal processes is a critical takeaway. The business landscape is dynamic, and the ability to pivot, innovate, and respond to changing circumstances is essential. This book encourages businesses to view their plans and proposals as living documents, subject to refinement and evolution.

Collaboration and communication emerge as recurring themes, underscoring the significance of teamwork and effective interaction in the planning and proposal phases. By fostering a collaborative environment within the organization and cultivating open lines of communication, businesses can harness the collective intelligence and creativity of their teams, leading to more robust plans and compelling proposals.

In addition, the integration of technology and data analytics in the planning process is crucial for businesses to stay competitive. Leveraging cutting-edge tools and technologies enables organizations to gather meaningful insights, streamline processes, and make informed decisions. This book advocates for embracing technological advancements as integral components of the business planning and proposal development toolkit.